KU-270-338

Did You Know?

CAMBRIDGE

A MISCELLANY

Compiled by Julia Skinner

With particular reference to the work of Clive Tully

THE FRANCIS FRITH COLLECTION

www.francisfrith.com

Based on a book first published in the United Kingdom in 2006 by The Francis Frith Collection®

This edition published exclusively for Identity Books in 2009 ISBN 978-1-84589-394-1

Text and Design copyright The Francis Frith Collection®
Photographs copyright The Francis Frith Collection® except where indicated.

The Frith® photographs and the Frith® logo are reproduced under licence from
Heritage Photographic Resources Ltd, the owners of the Frith® archive and trademarks.
'The Francis Frith Collection', 'Francis Frith' and 'Frith' are registered trademarks of
Heritage Photographic Resources Ltd.

British Library Cataloguing in Publication Data

Did You Know? Cambridge - A Miscellany
Compiled by Julia Skinner
With particular reference to the work of Clive Tully

The Francis Frith Collection
Frith's Barn, Teffont,
Salisbury, Wiltshire SP3 5QP
Tel: +44 (0) 1722 716 376
Email: info@francisfrith.co.uk
www.francisfrith.com

Printed and bound in Singapore

Front Cover: **CAMBRIDGE, SIDNEY STREET 1931** 84538p

The colour-tinting is for illustrative purposes only, and is not intended to be historically accurate

AS WITH ANY HISTORICAL DATABASE, THE FRANCIS FRITH ARCHIVE IS CONSTANTLY BEING
CORRECTED AND IMPROVED, AND THE PUBLISHERS WOULD WELCOME INFORMATION ON
OMISSIONS OR INACCURACIES

CONTENTS

INTRODUCTION

Cambridge is probably best known to many as a seat of learning,
but the history of the city - or town, as it was until 1951 - goes
back much further than the university colleges, and was founded
on principle's far more commercial than academic. Its major
importance was due to its position at the head of the navigation
on the River Cam, or Granta as it was known originally, making
it an ideal trading centre. When the college buildings did start
to appear, it was this position on the Fenland waterways which
allowed the extravagant use of building materials not usually
found in the region.

The first college to be founded was Peterhouse, by Hugh de
Balsam, the Bishop of Ely in the 13th century. Over the next 200
years or so, more colleges were added, and their power grew.
The university acquired the right to inspect weights and measures,
in order that traders would not take advantage of the students, and
the colleges even had their own courts, which could try offenders
against members of the university; not surprisingly, these powers
led to an uneasy relationship between 'town and gown'. While
monastic properties fell to Henry VIII's Reformation in the 16th
century, the colleges of Cambridge remained secure; in fact the
king even used the proceeds of dissolved religious establishments
to set up his own college, when he merged Michaelhouse and
King's Hall into Trinity College.

In recent years Science Parks have sprung up around Cambridge,
which is now recognised as one of the leading areas for computer
technology, and the airport has also brought added employment
to the area, which is now one of the most prosperous in the eastern
counties. During term time the streets of Cambridge are filled with
students on bicycles. Tourism is a major industry, and shops selling

Did You Know?
CAMBRIDGE
A MISCELLANY

postcards, souvenirs and fast food intermingle with academic bookshops, hotels and a large noisy market. The Strawberry Fayre each year and the Cambridge Folk Festival also attract a good following and bring many visitors to the city. However, Cambridge remains a pleasant place with a dignified charm, full of interesting corners and winding alleyways, all of which seem to end up at the River Cam.

The story of Cambridge is full of fascinating characters and events, of which this book can only provide a brief glimpse.

HOBBS'S PAVILION 1931 84523

Did You Know?
CAMBRIDGE
A MISCELLANY

CAMBRIDGESHIRE DIALECT WORDS AND PHRASES

In the 1950s a common phrase heard at Cambridge's cattle market was that a heifer (a young cow that had not yet calved) had *'been to the whist drive'* if it was suspected that she had actually had a calf. This implied that, like a young girl who had been out gallivanting, she was no longer the *'maiden'* she was supposed to be!

'Half the lies you hear aren't true.'

'Don't talk to strangers unless you know 'em.'

'Mizzle' - mist.

'It's wetted up outside' - it's rained hard.

'In and out like a dog at a fair' - being busy, hurrying about.

'Dockey' - the mid-day snack at work. It possibly gets its name from when wages were 'docked' for the time that workers took off for their meal break.

'Slubby' - runny mud.

'Ockered' - awkward or contrary.

'Backerds' - backwards.

'Thin as a yard of pump water' or *'straight as a pound of candles'* - describes someone very tall and thin.

An *'old boy'* is a young man, but a *'little old boy'* is an old man.

HAUNTED CAMBRIDGE

The Haunted Bookshop is reputed to have a ghost in residence upstairs, hence the name.

The ghost of Dr Butts, appointed Master of Corpus Christi from 1626, is said to haunt his old rooms at the college, in which he hanged himself on Easter Sunday 1632. The story goes that he had become depressed after a large number of students had died of the plague that year, writing to a friend that there was not an undergraduate to be seen in college or the town and that he was 'alone, a destitute and forsaken man'.

Another ghost story linked with Corpus Christi is about a 17th-century student who fell in love with a Master's daughter. Interrupted at a secret meeting, he hid in a kitchen cupboard and was suffocated, and returns to haunt the building.

Sightings of the supposed ghost of Dr Wood, who became Master of St John's before his death in 1839, have been reported on a staircase of the college. He is said to appear as the poverty-stricken student of his earlier years, when he used to wrap his feet in straw each evening to keep them warm and study by the light of the candle that lit the staircase.

Merton Hall, which belongs to St John's, was once said to be haunted by a strange 'penguin-like' creature, which has more recently also been seen moving along Newmarket Road. The phenomenon was examined by a local paranormal group, which concluded that the ghost might actually be that of a 'plague doctor', who was wearing a cloak and the beak-like mask which was believed to offer some protection against catching the plague in the 17th century.

The 16th-century Abbey House, which stands on the site of Barnwell Priory, was at one time noted for an exceptional array of ghosts, which included the ghost of a man, a white lady (assumed to be a nun), a rabbit referred to as 'Wolfie', a disembodied head, a clanking chain, the sound of rustling clothes and a poltergeist.

CAMBRIDGE MISCELLANY

The first major settlement of the Cambridge area probably began with the Roman invasion of Britain in the 1st century AD. A military outpost and associated settlement was established here around Castle Hill from which to defend the River Cam, and this was also the crossing point for the Roman road which linked Colchester in Essex with the garrisons at Lincoln and the north. The Roman settlement appears to have been inhabited until about AD400.

At the Peace of Wedmore in AD878 between the Danes and the Anglo-Saxon King Alfred, the two sides agreed to split the country into two areas of control. Grantebrycge (Cambridge) was absorbed into the Danelaw, the part of the country in which the Danes were allowed to settle and Danish laws, not Anglo-Saxon, were followed. The Danes settled mainly to the south of modern Quayside, and the period of Danish rule lasted for about 40 years. King Alfred's son and successor, Edward the Elder, re-conquered most of the Danelaw, and the people of Grantebrycge swore allegiance to him in AD921.

In 1209 a group of scholars came to Cambridge from Oxford, after having to leave in a hurry following a spot of trouble: some of their number had been accused of murder and were hanged in Oxford by the townspeople, with the approval of King John. While many of them returned to Oxford five years later when the fuss had died down, enough of them remained in Cambridge to form a scholastic community. By the mid 13th century, this gathering of students and teachers was recognised as a university, despite the fact that they had no buildings of their own. In 1284, the first college was built next to a church dedicated to St Peter, and was duly named Peterhouse by its founder, Hugh de Balsam, the Bishop of Ely.

PETERHOUSE 1890 26585

Peterhouse (see photograph 26585, above) is distinguished as Cambridge's first college, although the original 13th-century buildings have been altered considerably. Matthew Wren, uncle of the more famous Christopher, was Master here from 1625-34, and he was responsible for the chapel, which combines Perpendicular and Classical styles.

For many centuries, Oxford and Cambridge were England's only universities. In medieval times, students would enter the university at the age of fourteen, and stay until they were twenty-one, or sometimes older. The minimum seven-year course culminated in an MA or BA degree. Before there were any college buildings, the tutors lectured in borrowed halls and churches while their students took what lodgings they could in the town.

Amongst the treasures of King's College Chapel are the largest and most complete set of ancient windows in the world, and Rubens's masterpiece, 'The Adoration of the Magi', which is displayed behind the altar.

On the right-hand side of the road in photograph 60871, below, is First Court, the entrance to Christ's College, founded in 1505 by Lady Margaret Beaufort, the mother of Henry VII, whose arms and statue are displayed on the main gate. On the other side of the road is the Church of St Andrew the Great, which contains a monument to the explorer Captain Cook, along with the graves of his widow and two sons, the younger of whom attended Christ's College until he died of scarlet fever.

ST ANDREW'S STREET 1908 60871

THE EIGHTS 1909 61510

Cambridge has a long history of rowing, as both a leisure and a sporting activity. Because the River Cam is not wide enough for conventional races, races called 'Bumps' are held. Eights such as the one seen in this photograph start off some 1½ lengths behind one another, and each boat has to catch up with the one in front, 'bumping' it.

Cambridge's first women's college started in Hitchin in 1869, and moved to Girton three years later - sufficiently far removed from Cambridge and the temptations of its male students. But while the red-brick buildings seen in photograph 88501, above, offered women a higher education, it was to be another twenty years before women became entitled to receive degrees.

William the Conqueror built a castle at Cambridge in 1068 as a forward position for his campaign against Hereward the Wake, leader of a guerrilla campaign in the fenlands against the Normans. Nevertheless, Hereward fought on for another three years from his base in the Isle of Ely before finally being overcome. Only the original earth mound is left of Cambridge's castle; after 1400, references to it in documents are scarce, and by the 16th century it was described as 'utterley ruinated'.

Buried under Midsummer Common in large mass graves are Cambridge's early plague victims. Burials from the outbreak of the plague in 1665 were buried at Coldham's Common.

Joining the two courts of St John's College on either side of the River Cam is the Bridge of Sighs, shown in photograph 26449, below. It borrows the idea of the covered bridge from one of the same name in Venice. Although the Cambridge version, built in 1831, has barred unglazed windows, the students passing through it were not necessarily looking their last upon the outside world, as Lord Byron romanticised that the condemned prisoners were who used the original Venetian bridge.

THE BRIDGE OF SIGHS 1890 26449

The Church of the Holy Sepulchre in Bridge Street is one of only four round churches remaining in England; it was founded in 1130 by the Knights Templar on the model of the Church of the Holy Sepulchre in Jerusalem. It is usually referred to in Cambridge as the Round Church.

In the 15th century the Royal College of the Blessed Virgin Mary and St Nicholas of Canterbury, subsequently known as King's College, was founded by Henry VI. He had already set up Eton College in Windsor, and the new college would have its scholars drawn from there. As with Eton, the king's first concern was with the establishment of a chapel. Its design would be modelled more on the lines of a cathedral choir than the buildings typical of college chapels so far - this was the reason why the king's master mason, Reginald of Ely, was appointed as architect. Building started in 1446, but came to a premature halt with the Wars of the Roses; after the death of Henry VI, it fell to Edward IV, and later Henry VII, to continue the building, with Henry VIII overseeing the finishing touches in 1513.

Of the many Cambridge men who sailed to America in the 17th century, one was John Harvard, a graduate of Emmanuel College. He died in Massachusetts, leaving half his estate to a school which had just been set up in Newetowne, which was subsequently renamed Cambridge in commemoration of the place where around 70 of the colony's founders had been educated. The following year the school was named Harvard in his honour, and became Harvard College, one of the most prestigious colleges in the USA.

THE CHURCH OF THE HOLY SEPULCHRE
1890 26524

ST JOHN'S COLLEGE AND WREN'S BRIDGE c1955 C14021

Photograph C14021, above, shows Wren's Bridge at St John's College, built by Robert Rumbold in 1709-12. The bridge has a balustraded parapet and heraldic beasts on display. It is also known as Kitchen Bridge - it seems that the master and fellows of St John's defied the architect and had it put at the end of the lane leading to the college kitchens.

One of Cambridge's local legends is the story about the stone lions which flank the entrance to the Fitzwilliam Museum in Trumpington Street. According to different versions of the tale, when the clock of the nearby church strikes midnight, the lions either roar, come down to get a drink from the Trumpington Street gutters, or leave their plinths and go inside the museum.

In a commentary on the Oxford-Cambridge Boat Race in 1983, John Snagge famously remarked that the fog meant that he could not see who was in the lead, but it was either Oxford or Cambridge. He was unaware of making this gaffe until he heard a recording later!

Photograph 26568, below, shows Clare College from Clare Bridge, which dates from 1640 and is the oldest surviving bridge in Cambridge. This bridge was built in the classical style by Thomas Grumbold. The reason for this being the oldest bridge is that all the other contemporary bridges in Cambridge were destroyed by Parliamentarian forces during the Civil War, to make the town more defensible.

CLARE COLLEGE 1890 26568

Boating and punting on the Cam has long been a popular
pastime, but there is a real art to punting: if you do it properly,
both forward motion and steering is provided by the pole, but
it does take some practice. These days, gravel prevents the less

experienced punter from having his pole stuck in the mud. When the colleges enclosed the Backs, the towpaths became obstructed; gravel was spread on the bed of the River Cam so that horses towing barges could wade up the river instead.

THE CAM, TRINITY BRIDGE 1914 66902a

HILLS ROAD WAR MEMORIAL 1923 73559

TO THE MEN OF CAMBRIDGESHIRE
THE ISLE OF ELY, THE BOROUGH
AND UNIVERSITY OF CAMBRIDGE
WHO SERVED IN THE GREAT WAR
1914 - 1919

20

The War Memorial in Hills Road, shown in photograph 73559, opposite, is by Tait Mackenzie (1922). Prominently sited at a crossroads, the memorial is dedicated to the 'Men of Cambridgeshire, the Isle of Ely, the Borough and University of Cambridge'. The unusually informal and naturalistic design represents a bare-headed, long-striding soldier, and is titled 'Coming Home'.

The Cambridge and County Folk Museum is housed in the former White Horse Inn on Castle Street. It is one of the oldest social history museums in the country, and themed rooms show different aspects of life in Cambridgeshire in the past. The collection of folklore items is of national significance; many of these items were collected by the late Enid Porter, author of 'Cambridgeshire Customs and Folklore', who was a former curator of the museum. Amongst the items of interest in the museum are many objects associated with childhood, ranging from items connected with the rearing of children, such as nursery furniture and clothing, to toys and games. The museum also possesses a delightful and important collection of dolls' houses and a good range of dolls.

The sundial in the Old Court at Queens' College is one of the finest examples of sundial art in the country, but is especially noteworthy because it is also one of the very few moondials in existence. The shadow cast on the golden Roman numerals tells apparent solar time, and the table of figures below the dial is an aid to telling the time by moonlight, providing the moon is strong enough to cast a reasonable shadow. The sundial can also be used to observe the altitude of the sun, the date and time of sunrise and sunset, and the sign of the zodiac in which the sun currently lies.

The last two lines of Rupert Brooke's poem, 'The Old Vicarage, Grantchester', have immortalised the church of this village a few miles from Cambridge:

> 'Stands the church clock at ten to three
> And is there honey still for tea?

It is believed that the clock was actually broken when the poet was living in Grantchester. For years after Brooke's death in the First World War, the clock was kept at ten to three as a memorial to him. The nearby Grantchester Tea Rooms houses an excellent collection of photographs and exhibits about the poet and his contemporaries.

Many American airmen were stationed around Cambridge during the Second World War. Some of them scorched their names and squadron names with cigarette lighters on to the roof of the one of the bars in the Eagle pub, just off King's Parade, and these can still be seen. The Cambridge American Cemetery and Memorial at Madingley, a few miles west of the city, was created on 30 acres of land donated by the University of Cambridge. Buried here are 3,812 American service personnel who died during the war, but on the Wall of the Missing, running from the entrance to the chapel, are inscribed the names of 5,126 Americans who also gave their lives in the service of their country, but whose remains were never recovered or identified. Most of those buried or commemorated here died in the Battle of the Atlantic or in the strategic air bombardment of north-west Europe.

Cambridge is famous for the large number of people in the city who prefer pedal power. The 2001 census found that a massive 25% of residents travelled to work by bicycle, giving the city the highest level of cycle use in the United Kingdom.

**GRANTCHESTER, THE CHURCH OF
ST ANDREW AND ST MARY 1929**
81771

ADDENBROOKE'S HOSPITAL 1938 88528

When Dr John Addenbrooke died in 1719, he left over £4,500 to build a new hospital. Photograph 88528, above, shows Addenbrooke's Hospital from the roof of the Fitzwilliam Museum in Trumpington Street. Cambridge's hospital today is a vast complex on the southern outskirts of the city, renowned for its skill in dealing with head injuries.

The shop now occupied by Bowns in Magdalene Street was once the Cross Keys Inn, and features some erotic carved wooden gargoyles which leave you in no doubt as to what went on in the inn!

CAMBRIDGE
A MISCELLANY

In Northampton Street and Magdalene Street is the best range of medieval houses and cottages in the city; the long range of two- and three-storied plastered and timbered houses reminds us of what medieval Cambridge would have looked like.

Photograph 26515, below, shows hansom cabs lined up on Senate House Hill, alongside the elegant Classically-styled Senate House, the 'Parliament' building for the university. Behind is Gonville and Caius (pronounced 'keys') College, the archway opening up into Tree Court. In fact, Dr John Caius, who re-founded the College in 1557, was a Norwich man whose family name was originally Keys; later it was Latinised, as was the fashion of the day.

CAIUS COLLEGE AND SENATE HOUSE 1890 26515

The curious Mathematical Bridge across the Cam, seen in
photograph C14080, below, is built on geometric principles and
was the first bridge in the world to be designed according to
a mathematical analysis of the forces within it. The bridge was

originally held together - so the story goes - without any fixing devices. Apparently when it was taken apart in 1867 to discover the principles upon which it was built, those who dismantled it could not reassemble it without the use of bolts.

THE MATHEMATICAL BRIDGE c1955 C14080

HILLS ROAD, THE ROMAN CATHOLIC CHURCH
1908 60869

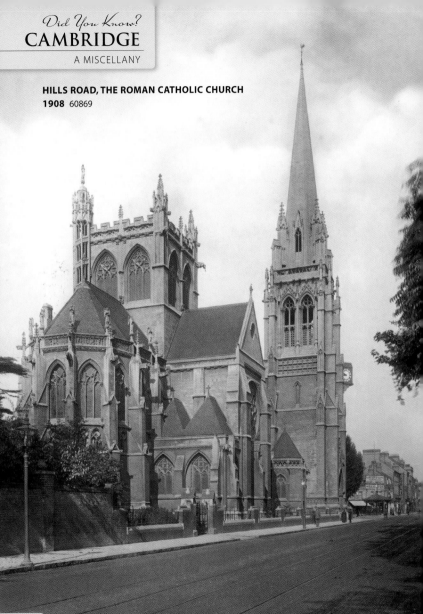

The earliest recorded reference to a bridge at Cambridge is in the 'Anglo-Saxon Chronicle' for AD875, when the Anglo-Saxon name for the settlement here is given as Grantebrycge. By Norman times the name of the town had become Grentabrige or Cantebrigge, while the river that flowed through it was still called the Granta. Over time the name of the town changed to Cambridge, but the river was still known as the Granta for a considerable period, and indeed is still often referred to as the Granta to this day. The name of the river was eventually changed to the Cam to be in line with the name of the town.

Many students who have passed through the university throughout the ages have helped shape events in history - among them are Oliver Cromwell, Samuel Pepys, Isaac Newton, Charles Darwin, Milton, Tennyson, Wordsworth and Byron. Oliver Cromwell, a student at Sidney Sussex College, later became the MP for Cambridge, and during the Civil War he made the town his headquarters for the Eastern Association. What is believed to be his embalmed/mummified head was buried in the ante-chapel of the college in 1960.

Not far from Pembroke College is Hobson's Conduit, named after a mayor of the city who had formerly run a livery stable and who inspired the phrase 'Hobson's Choice', because he refused to allow customers to choose their own horses - it was his choice, or none at all. Hobson's Conduit originally stood close to what is now the Guildhall, but was moved to its current site on Lensfield Corner when the Market Square was created. The railings around the conduit were where condemned criminals were tied and publicly whipped.

The people of the low-lying and damp fenlands of Cambridgeshire were very prone to rheumatic complaints in the past. One of the local folklore beliefs was that the condition could be alleviated by carrying the forefeet of a mole around in your pocket. Examples of these can be seen in the Cambridge and County Folk Museum on Castle Street.

The diaries of Samuel Pepys, the original manuscripts of which are in Magdalene College, contain the following comment on married life, which no doubt strikes chords of differing responses in husbands and wives everywhere:

'… my wife and I home and find all well. Only, myself somewhat vexed at my wife's neglect in leaving of her scarfe, waistcoat and night-dressings in the coach today that brought us from Westminster, though I confess she did give them to me to look after - yet it was her fault not to see that I did take them out of the coach.'
(Samuel Pepys, 'Diary', 6 January 1663.)

Magdalene College was founded by Henry VI as lodgings for student Benedictine monks, and was intended to be sited far enough from the town centre to prevent them falling prey to its temptations. It became a college in 1542. Samuel Pepys studied here between 1650 and 1653, and on his death in 1703 his library came here, including the original manuscript volumes of his famous diaries. The best-known Master of Magdalene College is A C Benson, who wrote 'Land of Hope and Glory'.

PETTY CURY 1931 84534

NEWNHAM COLLEGE, SEDGEWICK HALL 1890 26542

Newnham College was Cambridge's second college for women, and was built much closer to the centre of Cambridge than Girton. It originally started as just five women assembling in a house in Cambridge to be tutored by Mrs Jemima Clough; as the establishment grew, it moved into a building in the suburb of Newnham, taking that name for the college. When the Liberal politician W E Gladstone visited the college the occasion was celebrated with the planting of a tree, but shortly afterwards the sapling was uprooted by Tory undergraduates.

A tablet on one wall of the Old Court of Corpus Christi commemorates two of the College's most famous students, the Elizabethan dramatists Christopher Marlowe and John Fletcher.

The Fitzwilliam Museum in Trumpington Street contains Egyptian, Greek and Roman antiquities, oriental porcelain and ceramics, and important works of art; the nucleus of its outstanding collection of treasures was bequeathed by the 7th Viscount Fitzwilliam in 1816. The museum was described by the Standing Commission on Museums & Galleries in 1968 as 'one of the greatest art collections of the nation and a monument of the first importance'. Amongst its treasures are the sarcophagus lid of the Egyptian pharaoh Rameses III which was contributed by G B Belzoni; Islamic rugs, pottery and glass; the most complete collection of medieval British coins in existence; and an outstanding collection of medieval illustrated manuscripts.

THE FITZWILLIAM MUSEUM 1890 26605

33

Trinity College's Great Court, shown in photograph 66872a, below, was built between 1593 and 1615, and is the largest university quadrangle in Europe. The fountain in the centre was built at the beginning of the 17th century by Italian craftsmen.

TRINITY COLLEGE 1914 66872a

QUEENS' COLLEGE 1890 26572

Queens' College, shown in photograph 26572, above, was
founded in 1448. It was one of the first colleges to be built
in red brick at a time when the rather expensive fashion of
imported stone began to decline.

One of the most fascinating objects in the Cambridge and County
Folk Museum - and a salutary reminder of how our quality of life has
improved in modern times! - is a bed bug trap. This ingenious device,
made out of wickerwork, was used to catch the bugs which infested
beds in the past. It was placed behind the pillow, and before retiring
to bed you would remove the trap and shake out the bugs which
had crawled inside, thus (hopefully) guaranteeing yourself a bite-free
night's sleep.

Trinity College has a tradition known as the Great Court Run, which is an attempt to run round the perimeter of Great Court (a distance of approximately 367 metres) in the 43 seconds that the college clock takes to strike twelve o'clock. It is believed that the only two people to have actually completed the run in the required time are Lord Burghley, who did it in 1927 (see more information on page 38), and Sebastian Coe, who beat Steve Cram in a charity race in October 1988. Technically, Burghley was the second person to have completed the run in time, as someone had done it in the 1890s, but at that date the clock took five seconds longer to complete its toll. The challenge is only open nowadays to freshers, many of whom compete in fancy dress.

Jesus College grew from a 12th-century convent (see photograph 26530, below). James I visited the college, and was so impressed by its tranquil surroundings that he said, given the choice, that he would 'pray at King's, dine at Trinity and sleep at Jesus'.

JESUS COLLEGE 1890 26530

The building that now houses French Connection at Market Hill was a tobacconist's shop, Bacon's, from 1810 to 1983. Outside the shop is a large plaque inscribed with 'Calverley's Ode to Tobacco'. Charles Stuart Calverley (1831-84) was a fellow of Christ's College who was known for his eccentricity and his love of tobacco. This is a short extract from his ode:

> *I have a liking old*
> *For thee, though manifold*
> *Stories, I know, are told*
> *Not to thy credit!*

The first car to be driven in Cambridge was a Peugeot which was owned by the Hon C S Rolls (later of Rolls-Royce fame) while he was an undergraduate here.

Lord Burghley's successful attempt to race round the Great Court of Trinity College whilst the college clock tolled 12 o'clock was achieved in his final year at Cambridge in 1927. His feat inspired the scene in the film 'Chariots of Fire', in which the character of Lord Andrew Lindsay is loosely based on Burghley, although in the film the feat is actually achieved by Harold Abrahams - apparently that the film's director, David Puttnam, did not want to show a lord winning because of his socialist views, which was why Lord Burghley would not consent to his name being used in the film. The race scene in 'Chariots of Fire' was not actually filmed in the Great Court, but at Eton.

Cambridge boasts some interesting examples of unusual pillar boxes. A Penfold hexagonal pillar box can be seen on King's Parade, and there is an interesting spiked example on Priory Road - its purpose is unclear, but it was possibly originally sited near a garden wall, and the spikes may have been designed to deter people from using the pillar box to climb over the wall.

All Saints Passage in the Jewry is named after the church of All Saints which was demolished in 1865 as it jutted out over the pavement of Trinity Street, making it very narrow. The church was rebuilt on Jesus Lane; its position opposite Jesus College gave it the nickname of 'St Opposites'. The church, which has some interior decoration by William Morris, is now redundant and is used as an occasional venue for arts events.

MAGDALENE COLLEGE, THE PEPYSIAN LIBRARY 1890 26562

SPORTING CAMBRIDGE

Born in Cambridge in 1882, Sir John Berry 'Jack' Hobbs, the Surrey and England batsman, was undoubtedly the world's greatest cricket batsman of his time. Between 1905 and 1934 he played in 61 test matches and scored a record 61,237 runs. Perhaps his greatest innings at the Oval was against Australia in 1926, when he made a century to help bring back the Ashes to England. The list of his batting achievements is extensive but here are a few highlights: he scored 197 centuries in first class cricket, the most by any player in any country to date; he is the oldest man in cricketing history to have scored a test match century (at the age of 46); in 1953 he became the first professional cricketer to be knighted; and half his total of centuries were scored after the age of 40. In the year 2000, Wisden selected him as one of the top five players of the 20th century. Hobbs's Pavilion on Parker's Piece (shown in photograph 84523 on page 3 - note the batsman wind vane) honours Cambridge's sporting son. These days, Hobbs's Pavilion is a restaurant.

Cambridge United FC hold the distinction of winning the very first League play off final in 1990, to win promotion to Division Three. 1990-91 was also a fine year for the club. In the FA Cup they beat three Second Division sides, Wolves, Middlesbrough and Sheffield Wednesday. This was followed by a quarter final defeat at Arsenal in front of the London club's biggest crowd of the season. A fine run of eleven consecutive wins helped the team to promotion to Division Two.

One unwanted record that Cambridge United FC hold is that of going for 31 games without a win in 1984, still a record in the English professional game.

Cambridge United FC's best-known player is probably Dion Dublin. Dublin scored the goal that secured the club's promotion in 1990, and was a member of the following season's Division Three title-winning team. He was sold to Manchester United in 1992 for £1 million, and went on to play for England a number of times.

Nick Hornby, the author of 'Fever Pitch', was an undergraduate at Jesus College and a supporter of Cambridge United FC. Hornby records the habit of opposing team fans of gathering in the allotments adjacent to the Abbey ground and throwing cabbages over the stadium wall at the Cambridge fans.

Alistair Hignell is perhaps Cambridge's best known sportsman of recent times. He was born in Cambridge in 1955. After playing both rugby and cricket for Cambridge University he went on to play rugby for England and county cricket for Gloucestershire. Playing for Gloucestershire he once scored 100 in each innings against Surrey.

QUIZ QUESTIONS

Answers on page 48.

1. The Oxford-Cambridge Boat Race is rowed over a course of what distance?

2. Where in Cambridge can you see a Man Loaded with Mischief?

3. What is the link between Cambridge and Big Ben in London?

4. Over the medieval Great Gate of Trinity College is a statue of Henry VIII - why does the king hold a wooden chair leg?

5. Which student kept a pet bear with him during his time at Cambridge?

6. Cambridge became a city in 1951, but what was unusual about this event?

7. Cambridge is twinned with which two European places?

8. What is the link between Cambridge and the popular musical and film 'Grease'?

9. Who were the two queens commemorated in the name of Queens' College?

10. How did Portugal Place get its name?

THE RIVER CAM c1965 C14110

RECIPE

BURNT CAMBRIDGE CREAM

The recipe for Cambridge Burnt Cream is supposed to have originated at Trinity College in the 19th century.

Ingredients

600ml/1 pint double cream
1 teaspoon vanilla essence

4 egg yolks
3 tablespoonfuls sugar

Put the cream and vanilla essence in a saucepan and bring to the boil; meanwhile, in a large mixing bowl beat the egg yolks with 1 tablespoonful of the sugar until they are thick and pale yellow. Remove the cream from the heat and allow to cool slightly, then pour steadily over the egg yolks, whisking constantly. Transfer the mixture to an ovenproof dish or individual ramekins. Bake at 150 degrees C/300 degrees F/ Gas Mark 2 for about 30 minutes, until set. Leave to cool, then refrigerate for several hours.

About two hours before serving, preheat the grill to its highest temperature. Sprinkle the remaining sugar thickly and evenly over the surface of the cooked cream. Place the dish or ramekins under the grill, as close to the heat as possible, and allow the sugar to caramelise until a rich brown colour, but watching carefully to make sure that the sugar does not actually burn. Cool, and chill in the refrigerator again before serving so that the topping goes crunchy.

RECIPE

CAMBRIDGE SAUCE

Ingredients

6 hard-boiled eggs
300m/½ pint olive oil
4 anchovy fillets
2 tablespoonfuls mixed finely
chopped chervil, tarragon,
and chives

1 tablespoonful mustard
1 tablespoonful vinegar
1 teaspoonful capers
1 teaspoonful finely chopped
parsley
Cayenne pepper to taste

Blend the eggs, anchovy fillets, mustard, capers and mixed herbs
together into a smooth paste, using a food processor or pestle and
mortar. Slowly whisk in the oil and vinegar, and season with pepper.
Stir in the chopped parsley before serving.

QUIZ ANSWERS

1. 4½ miles.

2. At the Cambridge and County Folk Museum on Castle Street. The 'Man Loaded with Mischief' is on an inn sign, one of four such signs held at the museum which were painted by the local artist Richard Hopkins Leach in the 1840s.

3. The clock of Great St Mary's Church, the official University church, chimes a tune which was specially written for it in 1793, and which was later copied for Big Ben in London.

4. Many years ago, the sceptre held by the statue of Henry VIII above the Great Gate of Trinity College was replaced with a wooden chair leg as a student prank. It has remained there to this day. In the 1980s it was briefly replaced by a bicycle pump, but the chair leg was soon reinstated.

5. The poet Lord Byron. Byron had a noted fondness for animals from an early age, and his household always included a collection of unusual creatures as pets. Whilst Byron was a student at Cambridge he was annoyed that the university rules banned him from keeping a dog. With characteristic perversity, he installed a tame bear instead, arguing that there was no mention of bears in the statutes. The college authorities had no legal basis to complain, and the bear stayed until Byron graduated, when it went with him to his ancestral home at Newstead Abbey.

6. Cambridge was granted its city charter in 1951 even though it does not have a cathedral, which is usually a prerequisite for city status.

7. Cambridge is twinned with Heidelberg in Germany (1957) and Szeged in Hungary (1987).

8. The pop singer and actress Olivia Newton John, who played Sandy in the popular film of 'Grease', was born in Cambridge on 26 September 1948. She lived here until she was five, when her family emigrated to Australia.

9. Queens' College was first founded in 1448 by Margaret of Anjou, wife and queen of Henry VI, and then re-founded in 1465 by Elizabeth Woodville, wife and queen of Edward IV.

10. Portugal Place derives its name not from the country of Portugal, but from the port which was once shipped into Cambridge in vast quantities, brought by barges to the nearby Quayside, and taken from there to college dining tables.

KING'S PARADE 1921 70614

FRANCIS FRITH

PIONEER VICTORIAN PHOTOGRAPHER

Francis Frith, founder of the world-famous photographic archive, was a complex and multi-talented man. A devout Quaker and a highly successful Victorian businessman, he was philosophical by nature and pioneering in outlook. By 1855 he had already established a wholesale grocery business in Liverpool, and sold it for the astonishing sum of £200,000, which is the equivalent today of over £15,000,000. Now in his thirties, and captivated by the new science of photography, Frith set out on a series of pioneering journeys up the Nile and to the Near East.

INTRIGUE AND EXPLORATION

He was the first photographer to venture beyond the sixth cataract of the Nile. Africa was still the mysterious 'Dark Continent', and Stanley and Livingstone's historic meeting was a decade into the future. The conditions for picture taking confound belief. He laboured for hours in his wicker dark-room in the sweltering heat of the desert, while the volatile chemicals fizzed dangerously in their trays. Back in London he exhibited his photographs and was 'rapturously cheered' by members of the Royal Society. His reputation as a photographer was made overnight.

VENTURE OF A LIFE-TIME

By the 1870s the railways had threaded their way across the country, and Bank Holidays and half-day Saturdays had been made obligatory by Act of Parliament. All of a sudden the working man and his family were able to enjoy days out, take holidays, and see a little more of the world.

With typical business acumen, Francis Frith foresaw that these new tourists would enjoy having souvenirs to commemorate their days out. For the next thirty years he travelled the country by train and by pony and trap, producing fine photographs of seaside resorts and beauty spots that were keenly bought by millions of Victorians. These prints were painstakingly pasted into family albums and pored over during the dark nights of winter, rekindling precious memories of summer excursions. Frith's studio was soon supplying retail shops all over the country, and by 1890 F Frith & Co had become the greatest specialist photographic publishing company in the world, with over 2,000 sales outlets, and pioneered the picture postcard.

FRANCIS FRITH'S LEGACY

Francis Frith had died in 1898 at his villa in Cannes, his great project still growing. By 1970 the archive he created contained over a third of a million pictures showing 7,000 British towns and villages.

Frith's legacy to us today is of immense significance and value, for the magnificent archive of evocative photographs he created provides a unique record of change in the cities, towns and villages throughout Britain over a century and more. Frith and his fellow studio photographers revisited locations many times down the years to update their views, compiling for us an enthralling and colourful pageant of British life and character.

We are fortunate that Frith was dedicated to recording the minutiae of everyday life. For it is this sheer wealth of visual data, the painstaking chronicle of changes in dress, transport, street layouts, buildings, housing and landscape that captivates us so much today, offering us a powerful link with the past and with the lives of our ancestors.

Computers have now made it possible for Frith's many thousands of images to be accessed almost instantly. The archive offers every one of us an opportunity to examine the places where we and our families have lived and worked down the years. Its images, depicting our shared past, are now bringing pleasure and enlightenment to millions around the world a century and more after his death.

For further information visit: www.francisfrith.com

INTERIOR DECORATION

Frith's photographs can be seen framed and as giant wall murals in thousands of pubs, restaurants, hotels, banks, retail stores and other public buildings throughout Britain. These provide interesting and attractive décor, generating strong local interest and acting as a powerful reminder of gentler days in our increasingly busy and frenetic world.

FRITH PRODUCTS

All Frith photographs are available as prints and posters in a variety of different sizes and styles. In the UK we also offer a range of other gift and stationery products illustrated with Frith photographs, although many of these are not available for delivery outside the UK – see our web site for more information on the products available for delivery in your country.

THE INTERNET

Over 100,000 photographs of Britain can be viewed and purchased on the Frith web site. The web site also includes memories and reminiscences contributed by our customers, who have personal knowledge of localities and of the people and properties depicted in Frith photographs. If you wish to learn more about a specific town or village you may find these reminiscences fascinating to browse. Why not add your own comments if you think they would be of interest to others? See **www.francisfrith.com**

PLEASE HELP US BRING FRITH'S PHOTOGRAPHS TO LIFE

Our authors do their best to recount the history of the places they write about. They give insights into how particular towns and villages developed, they describe the architecture of streets and buildings, and they discuss the lives of famous people who lived there. But however knowledgeable our authors are, the story they tell is necessarily incomplete.

Frith's photographs are so much more than plain historical documents. They are living proofs of the flow of human life down the generations. They show real people at real moments in history; and each of those people is the son or daughter of someone, the brother or sister, aunt or uncle, grandfather or grandmother of someone else. All of them lived, worked and played in the streets depicted in Frith's photographs.

We would be grateful if you would give us your insights into the places shown in our photographs: the streets and buildings, the shops, businesses and industries. Post your memories of life in those streets on the Frith website: what it was like growing up there, who ran the local shop and what shopping was like years ago; if your workplace is shown tell us about your working day and what the building is used for now. Read other visitors' memories and reconnect with your shared local history and heritage. With your help more and more Frith photographs can be brought to life, and vital memories preserved for posterity, and for the benefit of historians in the future.

Wherever possible, we will try to include some of your comments in future editions of our books. Moreover, if you spot errors in dates, titles or other facts, please let us know, because our archive records are not always completely accurate—they rely on 140 years of human endeavour and hand-compiled records. You can email us using the contact form on the website.

Thank you!

For further information, trade, or author enquiries
please contact us at the address below:

**The Francis Frith Collection, Frith's Barn, Teffont,
Salisbury, Wiltshire, England SP3 5QP.**
Tel: +44 (0)1722 716 376 Fax: +44 (0)1722 716 881
e-mail: sales@francisfrith.co.uk **www.francisfrith.com**